W9-CIL-805

CUB REPORTER
MEETS FAMOUS AMERICANS

WHAT'S YOUR STORY, AMELIA EARHART?

Jen Barton
illustrations by Doug Jones

Lerner Publications ◆ Minneapolis

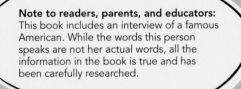

Note to readers, parents, and educators:
This book includes an interview of a famous American. While the words this person speaks are not her actual words, all the information in the book is true and has been carefully researched.

Lerner Publications Company
A division of Lerner Publishing Group, Inc.
241 First Avenue North
Minneapolis, MN 55401 USA

For reading levels and more information, look up this title at www.lernerbooks.com.

Main body text set in Avenir LT Pro 45 Book 15/21. Typeface provided by Linotype AG.

Library of Congress Cataloging-in-Publication Data

Barton, Jen.
     What's your story, Amelia Earhart? / by Jen Barton.
          pages cm. — (Cub reporter meets famous Americans)
     ISBN 978-1-4677-8783-3 (lb : alk. paper) — ISBN 978-1-4677-9645-3 (pb : alk. paper) — ISBN 978-1-4677-9646-0 (eb pdf)
     1. Earhart, Amelia, 1897–1937—Juvenile literature. 2. Women air pilots—United States—Biography—Juvenile literature. 3. Air pilots—United States—Biography—Juvenile literature. I. Title.
TL540.E3B37 2016
629.13092—dc23 [B]   2015000972

Manufactured in the United States of America
1 – VP – 12/31/15

Table of Contents

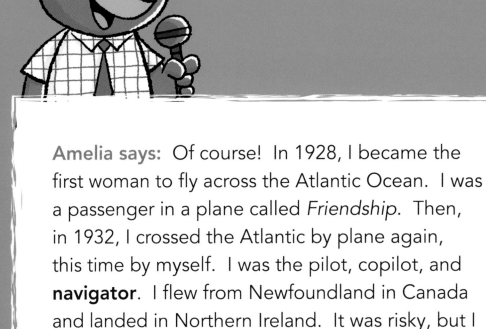

Hi, friends! Today I'm talking to Amelia Earhart. She is one of the world's most famous pilots. Amelia, we'd love to learn more about your life. Would you tell us about yourself?

Amelia says: Of course! In 1928, I became the first woman to fly across the Atlantic Ocean. I was a passenger in a plane called *Friendship*. Then, in 1932, I crossed the Atlantic by plane again, this time by myself. I was the pilot, copilot, and **navigator**. I flew from Newfoundland in Canada and landed in Northern Ireland. It was risky, but I had to follow my dreams. I also wanted to prove that women could be great pilots, just like men.

Amelia Earhart looks out from the door of an airplane in 1936.

Where and when were you born?

Amelia says: I was born in Atchison, Kansas, in 1897. At that time and place, girls weren't expected to be adventurous. They were expected to stay home and be **obedient**. But I loved adventure. I wanted an exciting life, like characters I'd read about in books.

I didn't see my first plane until I was twelve years old. Planes weren't common in the early 1900s. In 1920, I finally rode in a plane myself. And once I did, I was hooked! I knew I wanted to be a pilot.

Amelia *(left)* plays with her sister, Muriel, in the early twentieth century.

Amelia poses for a portrait at the age of ten.

How did you learn to fly?

Amelia says: I started taking lessons from a great female pilot named Neta Snook. My parents agreed that I could learn to fly if I had a female **instructor**. I took a job in the mailroom of a phone company to help pay for my lessons. The lessons were expensive, but they were worth it. Neta taught me everything she knew. We became close friends.

Soon I wanted a plane I could call my own. I saved up my money and bought one that was painted bright yellow! I named my plane *Canary*.

Neta Snook *(left)* stands with Amelia in front of Amelia's plane, *Canary*, on July 16, 1921.

How was flying
in your time different
than it is today?

Amelia says: When I flew, airplanes had been around for only a few years. Planes were smaller, and many **cockpits** were open to the sky. Sometimes I wore goggles to protect my eyes from the wind.

Safety was a main focus for **engineers**, mechanics, and early pilots like me. We dreamed of a time when flying would be as safe as it is today. Engineers and mechanics worked together to build safer planes and to keep them running smoothly. And pilots shared all we learned about planes with those who built them. That way, they could keep improving planes for future pilots.

Flying safely was important to Amelia. She often wore a cap to cover her ears and goggles to protect her eyes.

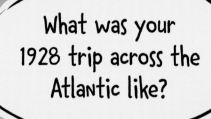

What was your 1928 trip across the Atlantic like?

Amelia says: It was thrilling and a little scary. Many people disappeared or died trying to take that same trip. But Bill Stultz was our pilot, and he was good! He flew us from Newfoundland to Wales in the United Kingdom. The flight was very cold. The plane's **cabin** wasn't heated like cabins are today. I had to wear a fur-lined suit over my clothes to keep warm.

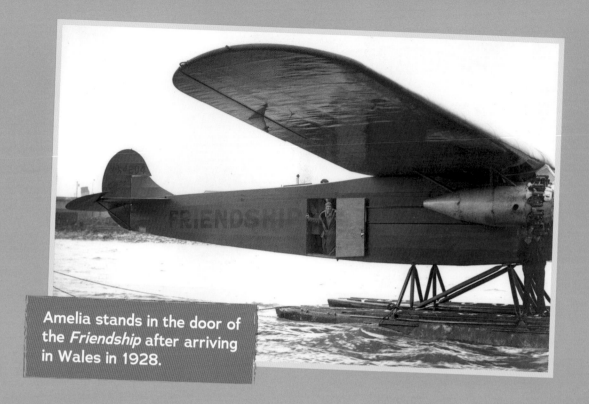

Amelia stands in the door of the *Friendship* after arriving in Wales in 1928.

Amelia *(center)* poses in her fur-lined suit for a photo with Bill Stultz *(right)* and his copilot, Lou Gordon, after their trip across the Atlantic.

Why did you make that dangerous journey?

Amelia says: I wanted to be the first woman to take on the challenge. I was proud when I met my goal. And I don't want to brag, but others seemed proud of me too. After the flight, I was famous. People said I was like Charles Lindbergh, the first person to fly **solo** across the Atlantic. They even called me Lady Lindy! But I still wanted to prove myself as a pilot. I wanted to be the first woman to cross the Atlantic alone.

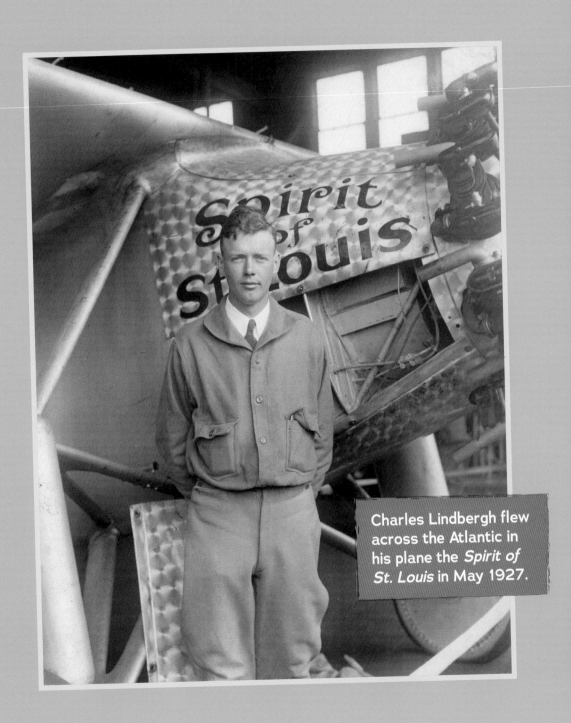

Charles Lindbergh flew across the Atlantic in his plane the *Spirit of St. Louis* in May 1927.

How did you prepare for your 1932 solo trip?

Amelia says: I added more fuel tanks and a new engine to my plane. I practiced new ways of navigating through fog. And I packed my favorite foods—tomato juice, chocolate, and raisins. But I kept my plans a secret. I didn't even tell my family. Other female pilots were preparing to cross the Atlantic, and I didn't want them to beat me!

A mechanic performs safety checks on Amelia's Lockheed Vega plane before her 1932 solo trip.

What happened on the flight?

Amelia says: On my way across the Atlantic from Newfoundland, I ran into a storm. Some of my equipment failed. The wings on my plane got icy. I had to fly lower into warmer air to melt the ice. But that put me close to the waves and water. Through it all, I stayed calm and kept on flying. Finally, I landed in a farmer's pasture in Northern Ireland.

A crowd cheers after Amelia's arrival in Northern Ireland on May 21, 1932.

How did people react to your trip?

Amelia says: I became even more famous. I gave speeches and lectures all around the United States. I spoke about **aviation** and women's rights.

I was invited to dinner at the White House. President Herbert Hoover presented me with the Gold Medal of the National Geographic Society. This award goes to people who make achievements in **geography**, or the study of where things are located. I was the first woman to ever receive that honor.

The city of New York threw a parade when Amelia returned from her trip. She was invited to give speeches and receive medals all across the United States.

What other records did you break during your life?

Amelia says: My very first record was in 1922, when I was twenty-five. I became the first woman to reach an **altitude** of 14,000 feet (4,267 meters). In 1935, I became the first person to fly from Hawaii to California. That same year, I flew solo from Los Angeles to Mexico City, which no one else had done. Meeting all these challenges was very satisfying for a pioneering pilot like me.

Amelia hands off a barograph after a flight in 1931. This device is used to measure a plane's altitude during flight.

Are there any honors you're especially proud of?

Amelia says: Yes! The United States Congress awarded me the Distinguished Flying Cross in 1932. The medal goes to people who've showed heroism or achieved something special in the field of aviation. I was thrilled to get that award. That year, I also received a trophy naming me America's Outstanding Airwoman. I was really proud of that because I'd always wanted to show that women could be great at flying. I won that trophy for the next two years as well. That meant a lot to me.

Vice President Charles Curtis *(left)* presents Amelia with the Distinguished Flying Cross on July 29, 1932. Amelia was the first woman to receive this medal.

How did you spend your time when you weren't flying?

Amelia says: I kept busy in lots of ways! I served as a nurse's aide in Canada during World War I (1914–1918). I helped care for wounded soldiers. I worked with kids in Boston at a place called Denison House. That was a home where poor people could live or visit to get free milk or coal to heat their homes. Denison House had classes too. I taught kids English there. I loved it!

After my flight in the *Friendship*, I wrote a book called *20 Hrs., 40 Min.* That's how long the trip took. I also wrote for newspapers and magazines. Later, I even designed a line of clothing.

Amelia stayed busy when she wasn't in the air. She worked as a nurse, a teacher, a writer and a clothing designer.

How did your life and work make a difference?

Amelia says: After I made my flights, people saw that women could be pilots if they wanted to. They also saw that women could work outside the home. My speeches on women's rights helped other women believe in their dreams. They saw me following my dreams, and it gave them the courage to follow theirs too. I hope both men and women can learn from my story that no dream is too big to chase!

Timeline

1897   Amelia Mary Earhart is born in Atchison, Kansas.

1918   Amelia becomes a nurse's aide in Canada.

1920   Amelia flies for the first time as a passenger.

1921   Amelia takes her first flying lesson.

1926   Amelia moves to Boston and works with kids at Denison House.

1928   Amelia becomes the first woman to cross the Atlantic by plane.

1930   Amelia sets a women's speed record by flying 181.18 miles (291.5 kilometers) per hour.

1931   Amelia marries her publicist and promoter, George P. Putnam.

1932   Amelia becomes the first woman to fly solo across the Atlantic.

1937   Amelia and navigator Fred Noonan take off from Miami on an around-the-world flight. On the last leg of their trip, they disappear over the Pacific Ocean. Their plane is never recovered.

Glossary

altitude: height

aviation: the study of flying an airplane

cabin: the part of an airplane where passengers sit

cockpits: places in the front of airplanes where pilots and the crew sit

engineers: people who design and build machines or other products

geography: the study of where things are located

instructor: someone who teaches

navigator: a person who sets the route on a trip. Many navigators use maps and special instruments to help guide them.

obedient: willing to do what someone tells you to do

solo: alone

Further Information

Books

Gilpin, Caroline Crosson. *Amelia Earhart.* Washington, DC: National Geographic, 2013. See photos of Amelia and discover more fun facts about her life.

Meltzer, Brad. *I Am Amelia Earhart.* New York: Dial Books for Young Readers, 2014. Get to know Amelia as she follows her dream to become a pilot.

Silverman, Buffy. *How Do Jets Work?* Minneapolis: Lerner Publications, 2013. Amelia believed flying was here to stay— and she was right! Today we fly all around the world in jets. Read this book to find out how they work.

Websites

Federal Aviation Administration—Which Is Stronger, You or Air? https://www.faa.gov/education/student_resources/kids_corner /ages_5_9/you_or_air
Try this simple experiment to test the weight of air.

Time for Kids—a Famous First
http://www.timeforkids.com/photos-video/video/famous -first-31381
See live footage of Amelia in this short black-and-white clip.

YouTube—NewsPlayer, Amelia Earhart
https://www.youtube.com/watch?v=lJg_-IwsmBE
Hear Amelia talk about her 1932 solo flight across the Atlantic.

Index

Photo Acknowledgments

The images in this book are used with the permission of: Library of Congress, p. 5; The Schlesinger Library, Radcliffe Institute, Harvard University, pp. 7 (all), 9; © New York Times Co./Getty Images, pp. 11, 15; © H.F. Davis/Topical Press Agency/Getty Images, p. 13 (top); © Charles E. Brown/Royal Air Force Museum/ Getty Images, p. 13 (bottom); © Bettmann/CORBIS, pp. 17, 21, 23; © ullstein bild/Getty Images, p. 19; AP Photo, p. 25; © Hulton Archive/Getty Images, p. 27.

Front cover: © Pictures Inc./The LIFE Picture Collection/ Getty Images.